SCHIRMER'S LIBRARY
OF MUSICAL CLASSICS

Compositions for the Piano
FRÉDÉRIC CHOPIN

Edited, Revised, and Fingered by
RAFAEL JOSEFFY

Historical and Analytical Comments by
JAMES HUNEKER

G. SCHIRMER, Inc.

DISTRIBUTED BY

HAL•LEONARD®
CORPORATION
7777 W. BLUEMOUND RD. P.O. BOX 13819 MILWAUKEE, WI 53213

FRÉDÉRIC-FRANÇOIS CHOPIN

I

THE years are marching toward the three-quarter of a century mark since the Polish composer, Frédéric-François Chopin, died at Paris in 1849. As immortality goes nowadays his is a considerable one for a pianoforte composer. Music is an evanescent art. The idol of yesterday is stale today. Notwithstanding the enormous repertoire of the keyboard, more than half is become purely academic: music taught, played by students. The professional virtuoso is more limited in his selections for public performance than we like to believe: Bach to Liszt, with a Beethoven sonata as *pièce de résistance*; and Chopin—always Chopin, whether his poetry is apprehended by the pianist or not; Chopin is the inevitable name that figures at every successful recital. All-Chopin programmes fill concert halls. Thanks to this the old Chopin is gone for most of us. It is not that he is played too often, but that he is badly, sadly played. Nevertheless, he holds his own, and not Debussy nor the young Russians have shaken his hold on the affections of concert-goers. The reason is not far to seek: He is the greatest of all composers for his instrument, and latterly he has had assigned to him even a more commanding position in the history of art. This thesis I have maintained for decades, and not so long ago I read the mature judgment of Dr. Friedrich Niecks, formerly Reid Professor at the Edinburgh University and author of the most complete biography of Chopin, that he believed Chopin "to be one of the three most powerful factors in the development of nineteenth-century music; the other two being, of course, Beethoven and Wagner." This is rather startling for those who see in the Pole only a graceful, withal, morbid talent; but it is a just estimate and a contention that may be upheld by cogent argument.

During the last half of the nineteenth century two men became rulers of musical emotion, Richard Wagner and Frédéric-François Chopin. The music of the Pole is the most ravishing in the musical art. Wagner and Chopin; the macrocosm and the microcosm. Chopin, a young man, furiously playing his soul out upon the keyboard, the soul of his nation, the soul of his time, is the most individual composer who ever set humming the looms of our dreams. Wagner and Chopin have an emotional element in their music that is intenser than any other composer's. They voiced their age. Chopin is nearer the soil in the selection of forms, his style and structure are more naïve, more original than Wagner's; while his medium, less artificial, is easier filled than the vast, empty frame of the theatre. Through their intensity of conception both men touch issues, though widely dissimilar in all else. Chopin possessed greater melodic genius than Wagner, and equal harmonic genius, playing the pioneer to the German in a hundred instances; he made more themes, he was, as Rubinstein said, "the last of the original composers." But his scope was not scenic; he preferred the stage of his soul to the windy spaces of the music-drama. His is the interior play, the eternal conflict between body and soul. He viewed his art across his temperament. Yet from Chopin one does not get, as from Beethoven, the sense of spiritual vastness, of the over-arching sublime. There is the pathos of spiritual distance, but it is pathos, not sublimity. He recalls Keats and Shelley; above all, Shelley. Chopin is the color genius of the pianoforte, his eye is attuned to hues the most attenuated; he can weave harmonies as ghostly as a lunar rainbow. The literary quality is absent in his work, as is the ethical—Chopin may prophesy, but he never flames into the divers tongues of the upper heavens.

Chopin is not only the poet of the pianoforte, he is the poet of music, the most poetic among composers. Compared with him Bach seems a maker of solid polyphonic prose, Beethoven a scooper of stars, a master of growling storms, Mozart a weaver of gay tapestries, Schumann a romantic wanderer. Schubert, alone, resembles him in lyric prodigality. Both were masters of melody, but Chopin was the master-workman of the two, and polished, after bending and beating his theme, fresh from the fire of his forge. He knew that to complete his "wailing Iliads" the strong and cunning hand was necessary; and he also realized that nothing is more difficult for the genius than to retain his own gift. Of all natures the most prone to procrastination, pessimism and vanity, the artist is conquered by ennui. It is not always easy to flame at the focus, to burn fiercely with the central fire. Chopin knew this, therefore cultivated his ego. He saw that the love of beauty-for-beauty's sake was fascinating, but led to the way called madness. So he rooted his art in the earth of Poland. Chopin neither preaches nor paints; yet his art is decorative and dramatic—in the climate of the ideal. He touches life and its issues in Poland only; otherwise, his music is a pure æsthetic delight, an artistic enchantment freighted with no ethical or theatric messages. Just because he did not label his works with any but general titles, Ballades, Studies, Preludes, Scherzi, and the like, his music sounds all the better; the listener is not pinned down to any precise mood, the music being allowed to work its particular charm without the aid of literary crutches for unimaginative minds.

Heine wrote that "every epoch is a sphinx which plunges into the abyss as soon as the problem is solved." Born in the very upheaval of the Romantic revolution—a revolution, be it said, evoked rather by the intensity of its emotion than by the power of its ideas—Chopin was not altogether one of the insurgents of art. But his name was as the stroke of a bell for the Romanticists, though he remained aloof from them, his attitude, however, being sympathetic. Chopin was a Classicist without knowing it; he compassed for the dances of his land what Bach did for the fugue and choral. With Heine he led the spirit of revolt, but enclosed his note of agitation in a frame beautiful. The coloring, the rhythmic versatility, "the lithe perpetual escape" from the formal, deceived his critics, Schumann among the rest. Chopin was the last of the idealists, the first of the realists. His novel form, his linear counterpoint, misled the critics who accused him of lacking what is really one of his virtues. We now know that Schumann was the more romantic writer, his pages replete with formal defects, while, in comparison, Chopin was a purist, almost pedantic. He had no feeling for the epic, his genius was too concentrated, and though he could be furiously dramatic the sustained majesty of blank verse (the symphonic form) was denied. With musical ideas he was ever charged, but their intensity is parent to their brevity. And it must not be forgotten that with Chopin the form was conditioned by the idea. He took up the dancing patterns of Poland because they were in key with his vivid inner life; he idealized them, transformed them, achieving a bolder, lengthier phraseology and larger architecture in the Ballades and Scherzi, though their prolonged periods are more passionate than philosophical. Just when his individuality germinated, who may tell? In his early music are discovered the roots and fibres of Hummel and Field. His growth, involuntary, inevitable, put forth strange sprouts, and in the pianoforte, an instrument of two dimensions, he revealed a third, and his music deepened and took on strange colors. The keyboard had never so sung; he forged its formula. Chopin seldom smiles, and, while certain of his music is young, he does not arouse in the mind pictures of youth and its fatuous romances. His passion is mature, self-sustained and never at a loss for precise phrasing. As the man grew he laid aside his ornaments and garlands; his line became sterner, its traceries more Gothic. Bach he made his chief god, and within the woven walls of his strange harmonies he sings the history of his unhappy and convulsed soul.

In Chopin the feminine often prevails; it may be noted, however, that this quality is sometimes a distinguishing sign of masculine genius. When he unbends, coquets and makes graceful confessions, or laments in lyric loveliness over fate, his mother's sex peeps out, a very picture of the beautiful, capricious Polish woman. When he stiffens the sinews of his soul, when Russia gets into his nostrils, then the smoke and flame of his Polonaises, the tantalizing despair of his Mazurkas, are testimony to the strong man-soul in rebellion. That he could attempt far flights one may see in his B flat minor Sonata, in the Scherzi, in several of the Ballads, above all in the F minor Fantasy. In this last-named great work the technical invention keeps pace with the inspiration. It coheres. There is not a rift in the idea, not a flaw in the reverberating marble. If Chopin, diseased to the very door of death, could build such a palace of dreams, what might he not have dared had he been healthy? But from his misery came sweetness and strength, like honey from the lion. The last ten years of his existence he grew amazingly, grew with a promise that recalls Raphael, Mozart, Schubert, Watteau, Keats, Shelley, and the rest of the early slaughtered angelic choir. His flame-like spirit waxed and waned in the gusty surprises of a disappointed life. His music may not, despite its canonic classicism, conform to the standards of Bach and Beethoven, but apart from its interior message, its very externals are marvellous. Delicate in linear perspective, logical in architectonic, its color is one of its charms: I think the Polish element in his music has been over-stressed by sentimental writers. Chopin is great despite his nationality. His is not map-music like Grieg's. It is, to be sure, Polish, but it is also something more. Chopin was first a poet and then a Pole. Too much patriotism is read into his measures. In literature the "Thaddeus of Warsaw" pose is dead, but it has survived in all its native pulchritude in many of the Chopin biographies. Liszt, rather Liszt's Princess Wittgenstein, is to blame for the rhapsodies in their monograph, which George Sand truthfully described as "un peu exubérante." The greater Chopin, the new Chopin which we Chopinists believe will endure longest, is not the Chopin of the Waltzes, Nocturnes—interesting as they are—nor the tricksy, impish Mazurkas. His idolaters swear by the Fantasy, the Barcarolle, the F sharp minor Polonaise, the Fantaisie-Polonaise, also the one in E flat minor; we believe that no more inspired pages have been written than the D minor, F minor and B flat minor Preludes, and we admire without restriction the F minor Ballade, the F major-A minor Ballade (the second), the F sharp major Impromptu, the E flat minor Scherzo—from the B flat minor Sonata—and the B minor and C sharp minor Scherzi. These are the quintessence of Chopinism.

II

Chopin is the open door in music. Besides being a poet and giving vibrating expression to the concrete, he was a pioneer; pioneer because, while he had bowed to the tyranny of the diatonic scale, he knew the joys of the chromatic. It is curious that at one time Chopin was regarded as an amateur among musicians, not as a "practical" musician. They declared him an unparalleled virtuoso, but even to-day your pedantic musician raises supercilious eyebrows when Chopin is called "creative." A cunning fingersmith, a moulder of decorative patterns, a master at making new figures, all these are granted, but speak of Chopin as a path-breaker in the harmonic forest, as the forger of a melodic metal, the sweetest, purest in temper, and you are still regarded by many, critics and laity alike, as one askew in your judgment. Yet Chopin invented many harmonic devices; he untied the chord that was restrained within the octave, leading it into the dangerous, delectable land of extended harmonies. And how he chromaticized the rigid, prudish Garden of German harmony! How he moistened it with flashing, changeful waters until it grew bold and brilliant with promise! This is now a commonplace, yet it will bear reiteration.

Chopin is the musical soul of Poland; he incarnates its political passion. First a Slav, by adoption a Parisian, he remains the open door because he admitted into the Western world the musical ideas of the East; Eastern tonalities, rhythms, in a word, the Slavic, which was once anathematized by timid, old-fashioned critics as objectionable, decadent, and dangerous. He inducted Europe into the mysteries and seductions of the Orient. His music lies wavering between the East and the West and in it, despite Kipling, the two are made "twain." A neurotic man, his soul trembling, his sensibilities aflame, the offspring of a nation doomed to pain and partition, it was natural for him to go to France—Poland had ever been her historical client—the France that had overheated all Europe. Chopin, born after revolutions, the true child of insurrection, chose Paris as his second home. Revolt sat easily upon his inherited aristocratic instincts, and Chopin in the bloodless battle of the Romantics will ever stand as the protagonist of the artistic drama.

All that followed—the breaking up of the old hard-and-fast boundaries on the musical map—is due to the labors of Chopin. A pioneer, he was rewarded as such by polite ignorement or bland condescension. He smashed the portals of the convention that forbade a man baring his soul to the multitude; and the psychology of music is the gainer thereby. Chopin, like Velasquez, could paint single figures perfectly, but, unlike the great Spaniard, he was not in sympathy with massed effects. Wagner did not fail to profit by his incomparably drawn soul-portraits. Chopin taught his century the pathos of patriotism and he showed Grieg the value of national ore. He practically re-created the harmonic charts, gave voice to the individual, himself a product of a nation dissolved by overwrought individualism. Schumann assures

that "Chopin is the proudest and most poetic spirit of his time." His transcendental scheme of technique is the image of a supernormal conception. At times he almost robs music of its corporeal vesture and his transcendentalism does not lie alone in his striving after strange tonalities and rhythms, but in seeking the emotionally recondite, the spiritual light that never was on sea or land. Self-tormented, ever "a dweller on the threshold," he saw visions that outshone the glories evoked by hasheesh, and his nerve-tormented soul ground in its mills music "exceeding fine." He persistently groped at the hem of Beauty's robe, and never sought to transpose to tone the brutalities of life; for attempting this he critically reproved Schubert. But such intensity cannot be purchased except at the cost of breadth, and his picture of life is not so high, so wide and sublime as Beethoven's. Yet it is as inevitable, as sincere, and as tragically poignant.

One of the greatest among great pianists was Chopin. He played as he composed—uniquely. All testimony is emphatically affirmative as to this. Scales that were pearls, a touch, rich, sweet, supple and singing, and a technique that knew no difficulties; these were part of his equipment as a virtuoso. He spiritualized the *timbre* of his instrument till it became transformed into something rare and remote from its original nature. His *pianissimo* was an enchanting whisper, his *forte* seemed powerful by contrast, so numerous were the tonal gradations, so widely varied his dynamics. The fairy-like quality of his play, his diaphanous harmonies, liquid touch and pedaling, all were the work of a genius; and the appealing sentiment he infused into his tone gave his listeners a delight that bordered on the supernatural. So read the accounts professional and personal. There must have been a hypnotic quality in his performance that transported his audience as the poet willed. Indeed, the stories wear an air of enthusiasm that borders on the fantastic. Crystalline pearls falling on red-hot velvet—or did Scudo write this of Liszt?—infinite nuance, and the mingling of silvery bells and their overtones—these are a few of the least exaggerated similes. Did not Heine call Thalberg a king, Liszt a prophet, Chopin a poet, Herz an advocate, Kalkbrenner a minstrel, Madame Pleyel a sibyl, and Doehler—a pianist? The limpidity and ease of Chopin's playing were, after all, on the physical plane. It was the poetic melancholy, the imaginative lift, that were more in evidence than sensuous sweetness. We know that Chopin had his salon side when he played with elegance, brilliance and coquetry. But he also had dark moments when the keyboard was too small, his ideas too big, for utterance. Then he astounded, thrilled his auditors. They were rare moments. His mood-versatility was reproduced in his endless coloring and capricious, even perverse, rhythms. The instrument vibrated

[v]

with these new, nameless effects like the violin in the hands of Paganini. Chopin was called the Ariel, the Undine of the pianoforte. There was something imponderable, fluid, vaporous, evanescent, in his music as presented by himself that eluded analysis, and illuded all save stubborn and prejudiced critics. Possibly this novelty was the reason why he was regarded by many musicians—Moscheles, for example—as a gifted amateur, instead of what he really was—the most daring harmonist since Bach.

Chopin's elastic hand, small, thin, with lightly articulated fingers, was capable of stretching tenths with ease. For confirmation of this examine the first Study in C. His wrist was very supple. Stephen Heller said that "it was a wonderful sight to see Chopin's small hands cover a third of the keyboard. It was like a serpent opening its mouth, about to swallow a rabbit whole." He played the octaves in the A flat Polonaise with infinite ease, but *pianissimo*. However, in his music there are many pianists, many styles, and all are welcome if they are poetically musical, logical and sincere. Mikuli asserted that Chopin brought out an "immense" tone in *cantabile*. His tone, as a matter of record, was not small, though it was not the orchestral tone of our time. Indeed, how could it be, with the light action and tone of the French pianos built in the earlier half of the last century? After all, it was quality, not quantity, that Chopin sought and attained. Each of his ten fingers was a delicately differentiated voice, and these ten voices could sing like the morning stars.

Chopin's personality was pleasant and persuasive, without being so striking or so dramatic as Liszt's. As a youth his nose was too large, his lips too thin—the lower one protruding—for beauty. Later, Moscheles said that he looked like his music. Delicacy, a certain aristocratic bearing and a harmonious ensemble produced a most agreeable impression. "He was of slim frame, middle height; fragile but wonderfully flexible limbs, delicately formed hands, very small feet, an oval, softly outlined head, a pale, transparent complexion, long silken hair of a light chestnut color, parted on one side, tender brown eyes, intelligent rather than dreamy, a finely curved aquiline nose, a sweet, subtle smile, graceful and varied gestures." This precise description is by Niecks. Liszt said that he had blue eyes, but he has been overruled. Chopin was fond of elegant, costly attire, and was very correct in the important matter of studs, cravats and walking-sticks. Not exactly the ideal poet-musician we fancied, but a gentleman. Berlioz advised Legouvé to see and hear Chopin, "for he is something you have never seen—and some one you will never forget." Allied with such refinement was the habit of punctuality. His naturally dignified behavior was increased by constantly associating with polite society. He was an aristocrat, and he did not care to be hail-fellow-well-met with musicians. This attitude and a certain primness, even asperity, did not make him popular. When teaching his manner warmed, the earnest artist came to the surface, his halting speech and insincerities were abandoned. His pupils adored him. Here at least the sentiment was one of solidarity.

He was a remarkable teacher, though he never had but one genius, little Filtsch, a Hungarian lad of whom Liszt had said, "When he starts playing I'll shut up shop." Filtsch died at the age of fifteen (in 1845). Paul Gunsberg, who died the same year, was another talented youth. While he never had the pupils to mould as had Liszt, Chopin made some excellent pianoforte artists. They had his tradition (see Niecks for the list of names), but exactly what the Chopin tradition is no man may dare assert. Liszt, naturally, being nearer the original source, played Chopin as no one else, yet the Pole complained of the liberties that Liszt allowed himself with his text. I heard Rubinstein (Anton, not Nicholas) play much Chopin in his seven historical recitals; nevertheless a few of the old guard still hobbling about in Paris declined to accept the Russian lion, with the velvet paws, as an authentic interpreter. Georges Mathias, a genuine pupil of Chopin, a veritable walking treasure house of information, told me this. He considered that Rubinstein's touch was too full, too rich, his tone too big, too thunderous. The unearthly element in the music was absent in the noble, full-blooded treatment of the glorious Anton. I doubt if even Carl Tausig, impeccable artist, Pole, and master of exotic moods, would have altogether pleased the composer. Chopin was spontaneous and played as his fancy prompted, and his playing was the despair and delight of his listeners. Rubinstein did miraculous things with the *coda* of the Barcarolle, yet Charles Hallé said it was "clever but not Chopinesque." Hallé had heard Chopin at his last Paris concert, February, 1848, play the two *forte* passages in the Barcarolle "*pianissimo* and with all sorts of dynamic finesse." Von Bülow was too much the martinet to reveal the poetic quality, though he fully appreciated the intellectual aspects of Chopin; and then his touch was not beautiful, though, odd as it may seem, I heard him deliver the D flat Nocturne most eloquently. The Slavic and Magyar races are your true Chopin interpreters. Witness Liszt, the magnificent Rubinstein, a passionate genius, Tausig, who united in himself all the elements of greatness and elemental grandeur, Annette Essipova, fascinating and feminine, the poetic Paderewski, Pachmann the fantastic, the super-subtle magic-working Joseffy, Godowsky, whose performances of a New Chopin border on the miraculous, and Rosenthal, who thunders in the Polonaises and whispers in the lyric numbers.

The acoustic parallelisms of Chopin are not as vivid, as concrete, as Richard Wagner's; nor are they so obvious, so theatrical. However, it does not demand much fancy to conjure up "the dreams and tramplings of three conquests" in the Heroic Polonaise, the F sharp major Impromptu or the episode before the Mazurka in the Polonaise in F sharp minor. The rhythms of the Cradle Song and the Barcarolle are suggestive enough, and there are dewdrops in his cadenzas and whistling of the wind in the last A minor Study. Of the A flat Study Chopin said—so Kleczynski reports—"Imagine a little shepherd who takes refuge in a peaceful grotto from an approaching storm. In the distance the wind and the rain rush, while the shepherd gently plays a melody on his flute." There are word-whisperings in the F minor Study which follows (opus 25, No. 2); while the symbolism of the dance—Waltz, Mazurka, Polonaise, Menuetto, Bolero, Schottische, Krakoviak, Rondo and Tarantella—is admirably indicated in all of them. The bells of the Funeral March, the will-o'-the-wisp character of the last movement of the B flat minor Sonata, the dainty Butterfly Study in G flat (opus 25), the æolian murmurs of the E flat Study (opus 10), the tiny prancing silvery hoofs in the F major Study (opus 25), the flickering flame-like C major Study (opus 10, No. 7), the spinning in the D flat Waltz and the cyclonic rush of chromatic double-notes in the E flat minor Scherzo —these are not studied imitation, but spontaneous transpositions to the ideal plane of natural sounds.

Chopin founded no school, though the supreme possibilities of the pianoforte were canalized by him. In playing, as in composition, only the broad trend of his discoveries may be followed, for his was an individual manner, not a pedagogic method. He has had his followers: Liszt, Rubinstein, Mikuli, Zarembski, Nowakowski, Scharwenka (Xaver), Saint-Saëns, Heller, Scholtz, Nicodé, Moszkowski, Paderewski, Leschetizky, and a group of the younger Russians, Liadow, Arensky, and Scriabine —the latter particularly, who has assimilated Chopin in an amazing manner. Even Brahms— in his F sharp minor Sonata and E flat minor Scherzo (opus 5)—shows the influence of the Pole.

Indeed, but for Chopin much latter-day music would not exist. Edgar Stillman Kelley has completely shown, in his "Chopin the Composer," (G. Schirmer) the indebtedness of Wagner, both thematically and harmonically. Withal, there is no Chopin school. Henselt in only a German who fell asleep and dreamed of Chopin. To a Thalbergian euphony he added a technical figuration, at times not unlike Chopin's, and a spirit quite Teutonic in its sentimentality. Rubinstein calls Chopin the exhalation of the third epoch in art. He certainly closed an epoch, as did Wagner. With a less strong rhythmic impulse the music of Chopin might have degenerated into a perfumed impressionism, like the French school of to-day, with its devotion to cold decoration and morbid ornamentation. Mannerisms Chopin had—what great composer has not? But the Greek in him kept him from the cult of the ugly, the formless. He is seldom a landscapist, but he can handle his brush deftly in the presence of nature. He paints atmosphere, nocturnal open air, with consummate skill, and for playing fantastic tricks on the nerves in the depiction of the superhuman he has a peculiar gift. Remember that in Chopin's days the Byronic pose, the love of the horrible, the grandiose, prevailed; witness the pictures of Delacroix and Ingres; while Jean Paul Richter wrote with his heart saturated in moonshine and tears. Chopin did not altogether escape the artistic affectations of his generation. But he is a magician of fiery and crepuscular moods, the most magical mirror of music.

III

Of Chopin's life it may be said that he played, composed, and loved. His love for his family was later reincarnated in his passion for George Sand; his love for his country is vividly expressed in his music. Self-exiled, he never ceased to dream of Poland, and perhaps it might have conduced to his greater happiness if he had not left Warsaw for Paris. His was not a stirring existence; no triumphal tours à la Liszt tempted him from his laborious lesson-giving and composition. Buried in the pages of his music is his spiritual biography; in actual life he was a dreamer of dreams, a man for whom the invisible world existed. Born of mixed nationalities, there was a dissonance in his temperament—a temperament once described by his friend Liszt as "umbrageous"—which displayed itself in a profound ennui, dissatisfaction with the present, and a certain spleen. When he was in Paris he longed for Poland; in Warsaw he dreamed of Vienna or Paris. An enigma to his admirers, an enigma doubtless to himself, nevertheless Chopin was no sentimental dawdler. In the history of the Seven Arts it would be difficult to find a more painstaking worker. He never spared himself, and his days were laborious and crowded with ambitions not always realized.

He was born at Zelazowa-Wola, near Warsaw, Poland, March 1, 1809-1810. I give these conflicting dates because, while I believe the former to be correct, Mr. Paderewski and other authorities have assured me, however, that the latter is the real one. As I intend only to give a skeletonized version now of the life, therefore I need not re-argue an old case about which there is much to be said on both sides. Warsaw has imitated the date, 1810, which is on the tomb at Père-La-Chaise, Paris, so let the matter rest; though I may refer my readers to the magisterial work on Chopin by Professor Niecks. The father of Frédéric-François was a Frenchman from Nancy, Lorraine—probably of Polish origin—the mother of pure Polish blood, by name Justine Krzyanowska. George Sand said with her characteristic acuteness that his mother was the supreme passion of Chopin. It is true. Chopin was musically precocious and improvised at an early age. His first teacher was a Bohemian violinist in Warsaw, Adalbert Zwyny, and the lad went ahead so fast that in 1818 he played in public a pianoforte concerto by Gyrowetz. Later he had the good luck to have as a master Joseph Elsner, who, a severe disciplinarian, put his pupil through all the classical paces; and for his sound instruction Chopin was ever grateful. He was an industrious boy, practical in all that concerned his art, though so modest when he made his début that he told his mother the audience had applauded his new collar! Early he began experimenting with technical problems. He travelled but little; once to Berlin, and in 1829 to Vienna. Here, August 11th of that year, he made his first bow to the greater musical world, and with his Variations opus 2, on "Là ci darem la mano," he won his spurs. He went into society—Chopin always dearly loved a princess—was petted by the aristocracy, heard many singers and musicians of renown and did not fail to profit by his experiences. In the meantime he had fallen in love with Constantia Gladowska, a singer, and she, so he hints in a letter, inspired the F minor concerto, or at least its poetic Larghetto. Like Goethe, and many a lesser poet, Chopin transmuted his emotional adventures into the terms of purest art.

After playing several times in Warsaw the spirit of "divine discontent" seized him and he revisited Vienna during the summer of 1831. His love had not been successful, yet he contrived to enjoy himself, hearing the tenor Rubini, Henrietta Sontag, Hummel—whose influence is manifest in his early works—and Thalberg, then the lion virtuoso. When the Russians entered Warsaw, September 8th, 1831, Chopin was at Stuttgart and there penned, so it is said, his Revolutionary Study in C minor. October of that year saw him first in Paris, his future home and last resting-place, although his original intention was to remain there only a few months, thence to visit London, perhaps New York. But his unqualified triumph at the house of Baron Rothschild caused him to change his plans. Invitations poured in, he became the rage in fashionable salons, and if he had not been made of sterner stuff than is usually accredited him by sentimental writers he would have succumbed to flattery and degenerated into a drawing-room entertainer. Luckily such was not the case. He never came into actual rivalry with virtuosi like Liszt, Thalberg, Herz, Hiller, Kalkbrenner and others, for his public appearances were limited, his audience few and fit; but his playing was so original, his music so extraordinary, that he was spoken of as one of the elect. Liszt loved him, Heine wrote wonderful prose about him, while Berlioz and Meyerbeer admired but avowed they could not understand him. Then the lady with the "sombre eye," Madame Aurore Dudevant, known to the literary world as George Sand, appeared on the brilliant horizon of the deracinated Pole. They promptly fell in love; George Sand described her sentiments as "maternal," but for Chopin it was love, desperate, whole-souled, and, as events proved, fatal love. There is no need to rehearse the pros and cons of this famous affair, quite as famous as the earlier one, which embroiled George Sand with Alfred de Musset. Chopin was a "difficult" friend and lover, and then his health was always delicate; Madame Sand took him, in company with her two children, to Majorca, but his lungs were not healed. He confessed that the public suffocated him, and his concerts became rarer. He continued to give lessons to his more favored pupils, taking long vacations at Nohant, where Madame Sand had her country home. There were signs that the long friendship was about to be ruptured. He was a trying invalid, captious and exigent. Madame Sand has frankly told us (as a "literary lady" she was admirable in her utilization of every romantic incident of her life) that she became weary of his complaints and jealousy. They separated. It was, literally, his death-warrant. But he went his usual ways, composing, never saving money; though he never dissipated, never gambled (he gave too much to his Polish friends), and the last year of his life was devoid of adventure, save a visit to England and Scotland. The strain of travel and playing on his fast ebbing strength proved fatal. Chopin, long attainted, died of consumption at Paris, March 17, 1849. His funeral was, metaphorically speaking, the greatest triumph of his career. Since then his reputation has waxed and will continue to grow. Karaszowski, in his endeavor to escape Liszt's pen-portrait of a Camille of the keyboard, with violets, tears and tuberculosis, went to the other extreme, and in his biography gives us the picture of a possible Polish athlete. Neither study is true. Of all the Chopin biographers I prefer Niecks; though I hear that a writer, Hoesick by name, has published a monumental life in Warsaw that may prove a worthy companion to that of the Edinburgh biographer. After all, the best of Chopin is in his music.

THE WALTZES

Of the Chopin Waltzes I have said that they are dances for the soul, not the body. But their animated rhythms, insouciant airs and brilliant, coquettish atmosphere, the true ball-room atmosphere, seem to smile at this exaggeration. The Waltzes are the most objective of the Chopin works, and only in a few of them is there a hint of the spleen and melancholy of the Nocturnes and Scherzi. They are less intimate in the psychic sense, but are exquisite exemplars of social intimacy and aristocratic abandon. As Schumann declared, the dancers of these Waltzes should be at least countesses. Despite their intoxicating movement there is high-bred reserve, and never a hint of the brawling peasants of Beethoven, Grieg, Brahms, Tschaikowsky or Dvořák. Yet little of Vienna is in Chopin. About the measures of this popular dance he has thrown mystery, allurement and secret whisperings and in them there may be found an involuntary sigh. It is going too far not to dance to some of this music, thus barring Chopin from a world he loved. In reality, certain of the Waltzes may be danced: the first, second, fifth, sixth, and a few others; the dancing would be more picturesque and less conventional than demanded by the average Waltz, and there should be fluctuations in tempo, sudden surprises, abrupt languors. The Mazurkas and Polonaises are danced in Poland, why not the Waltzes? Chopin's genius reveals itself in these dance-forms, and their presentation need not solely be a psychic one. Kullak divided the Waltzes into two groups; the first dedicated to Terpsichore, the second frankly a frame for moods. Chopin admitted that he was unable to play a Waltz in the Viennese fashion, though he has rivaled Strauss in his own genre. Some of the Waltzes are poetically morbid and even stray across the border into the rhythm of the Mazurka. Nearly all of them have been reduced to the commonplace by trite methods of performance, but are altogether sprightly, delightful specimens of the composer's careless, vagrant and happiest moods.

(A work of warning here will not be amiss concerning the habitual neglect of the bass. It ought to mean something in Waltz tempo, but usually it does not. Nor need the bass be brutally banged: the fundamental tone must be cared for, the subsidary harmonies lightly indicated. The *rubato* in the Waltz need not obtrude itself too markedly, as for example in the Mazurka.)

The Waltz opus 18 in E flat was published June, 1834. It is a true ball-room picture in spirit and in rhythms infectious. Of it Schumann wrote rhapsodically. There is bustle and chatter in this Waltz; the D flat section has a tang of the later Chopin. In form and content it is inferior to opus 34, A flat. The three Waltzes of this set were published December, 1838. There are many editorial differences concerning the A flat Waltz, owing to the careless way it was copied. This Waltz could be danced to as far as its dithyrambic *coda*. The next Waltz in A minor has a tinge of Sarmatian melancholy; indeed, it is one of Chopin's most desponding moods. The episode in C rings of the Mazurka, and the A major section is of exceeding loveliness. Its *coda* is characteristic. This Waltz is a favorite. The F major Waltz, the last of the series, is wild and whirling. It has the perpetual movement quality, and older masters would have prolonged its giddy arabesque into pages of senseless spinning, though it is quite long enough as it is. The second theme is better, but the *appoggiaturas* are flippant. It buzzes to the finish. Of it is related that Chopin's cat, probably emulative of the fame of Scarlatti's, sprang upon his keyboard and its feline flight suggested to him the idea of the first measures. As there is a dog Waltz I suppose there had to be one for the cat. Not improvised in the ball-room as the preceding, yet a marvellous epitome, is the A flat Waltz opus 42, published July, 1840. It is the best-rounded specimen of Chopin's efforts in the form. The prolonged trill in A flat, summoning to the dance; the intermingling of rhythms, duple and triple; the coquetry, hesitations, passionate avowal, and the superb *coda*, with its echoes of the evening—have not these episodes a charm beyond compare! The D flat Waltz, "le valse du petit chien," is of course George Sand's own prompting. One evening at her home in the Square d'Orléans, Paris, she was amused by her pet dog chasing its tail. She begged Chopin (then her pet pianist) to set the tail to music. He did, and the world is richer for this piece. I do not dispute this story, it seems to be well grounded, nevertheless it is silly. The Waltzes of this opus 64 were published September, 1847. It is hardly necessary to add that the D flat Waltz has been and still is played to death. Even street organs drive its swift bars helter-skelter across their brassy gamuts. After Tausig played it in double-notes, George Sand might have said that she heard two little dancing dogs.

The C sharp minor Waltz, same opus, is the most poetic of all. The veiled melancholy of the first theme has seldom been excelled by the composer. It is a fascinating lyric sorrow, and the psychologic motivation of the first theme in the curving figure of the second theme does not relax the spell. A space of clearer skies, warmer, more consoling winds are in the D flat interlude; but the spirit of unrest soon returns. The elegiac note is unmistakable in this veritable soul dance. The next Waltz in A flat is charming. It is for superior beings who dance with intellectual joy; with the joy that comes of making exquisite curves and patterns. Out of the salon and from its brilliantly lighted spaces the dancers do not wander into the darkness, into the church-yards, as Ehlert imagines of certain other of these Waltzes. The two Waltzes in opus 69, three Waltzes, opus 70, and the two Waltzes respectively in E minor and E major, need not detain us. They are posthumous. The first of opus 69, in F minor, was composed in 1836; the B minor in 1829; G flat, opus 70, in 1835; F minor in 1843; and D flat major, 1830. The E major and E minor were composed in 1829. Fontana gave these compositions to the world. The F minor Waltz, opus 69, No. 1, has a charm of its own; it is suavely melancholy, but not as much so as the B minor Waltz in the same opus. In color this latter recalls the B minor Mazurka. Very gay and sprightly is the G flat Waltz, opus 70, No. 1. The succeeding in F minor reveals no special physiognomy, while the third contains germs of the opus 34 and opus 42 Waltzes. It also recalls the D flat Étude in the supplementary series. The E minor Waltz is beloved. It is graceful and not without sentiment. The part in the major is the early Chopin. The E major Waltz is rather commonplace, hinting of its composer only at intervals. Paradoxical as it may sound, these Waltzes prove Chopin to be the greatest French composer for the pianoforte, for there is no denying their Gallic grace and mundane atmosphere. They may not be Chopin's most signal success in his art, yet in them he has lent the wings of inspiration to a conventional dance-form.

James Huneker

25502

Thematic Index

WALTZES

A Laura Harsford

Grande Valse brillante

Revised and fingered by
Rafael Joseffy

.F. Chopin. Op. **18**

25502

25502

25502

25502

12

A Mademoiselle de Thun-Hohenstein

Valse brillante

Revised and fingered by
Rafael Joseffy

F. Chopin. Op. **34**, No. **1**

25502

15

À Madame G. d'Ivry

Valse brillante

Revised and fingered by
Rafael Joseffy

F. Chopin. Op. 34, No. 2

25502

A Mademoiselle A. d'Eichthal

Valse brillante

Revised and fingered by
Rafael Joseffy

F. Chopin. Op. **34**, No. **3**

Valse

Revised and fingered by
Rafael Joseffy

F. Chopin. Op. 42

A Madame la Comtesse Delphine Potocka

Valse

Revised and fingered by
Rafael Joseffy

F. Chopin. Op. **64**, No. **1**

Molto vivace

6.

leggiero

A Madame Nathaniel de Rothschild

Valse

Revised and fingered by
Rafael Joseffy

F. Chopin. Op. 64, № 2

Tempo giusto

7.

Klindworth:

A la Comtesse Katharina Bronicka

Valse

Revised and fingered by
Rafael Joseffy

F. Chopin. Op. 64, No. 3

Moderato

8.

25502

25502

poco a poco accel. al fine

Valse

(Posthumous)

Revised and fingered by
Rafael Joseffy

F. Chopin. Op. 69, No. 1

(1836)

9.

25502

Revised and fingered by
Rafael Joseffy

Valse
(Posthumous)

F. Chopin. Op. 69. No. 2
(1829)

10.

25502

25502

Valse

(Posthumous)

Revised and fingered by
Rafael Joseffy

F. Chopin. Op. **70**, No. **1**
(1835)

Molto vivace (♩.=88)

11

f brillante

Valse

(Posthumous)

Revised and fingered by
Rafael Joseffy

F. Chopin. Op. 70, No. 2

12.

25502

25502

Valse
(Posthumous)

Revised and fingered by
Rafael Joseffy

F. Chopin. Op. 70, No. 3

Moderato (♩ = 108)

13.

Valse
(Posthumous)

Revised and fingered by
Rafael Joseffy

F. Chopin

Vivace

14.

25502

25502

25502

Valse

(Posthumous)

Edited by Carl Mikuli

F. Chopin
(1829)

Tempo di Valse

15.

Note: **The authenticity of this Valse is questioned.**